CONOCIMIENTOS

PRESS

Feb. 2021

Maria

I hope you enjoy
rereading my book P.
true-life family stories.
(There's a few new ones)

love,
Helen

Grandpa Lee's Stories

NEW MEXICO
TO CALIFORNIA

Helen Najera Reyes

CONOCIMIENTOS
PRESS

Illustrations by Hector Garza

Published by Conocimientos Press, LLC
San Antonio, Texas

ISBN: 978-1-7351210-0-0

CONOCIMIENTOSPRESSLLC.COM

This book is for my grandchildren:
Ava and Gabriel Posada, Ariana and Maya Diaz,
twins Antonio and Joaquin Arguedas,
and our newest grandbaby,
Sarafina Luna Arguedas.

It is also for my dearly departed father
Frank Tornel Najera (August 13, 2014),
and my mother Lucy Maestas, whose
invaluable recollections of her New Mexico
childhood made this book possible.

And, most of all, to my grandfather,
Elizardo "Lee" Maestas,
lovingly remembered as Grandpa Lee.

Stories

the Maestas

Elizardo "Lee" ⌐ Anita

Phil
Agnes
Joe
Dora
Isidor
Anna
Lee
Lucy
Ralph
Beatriz

Grandpa Lee and the Family

THE MAESTAS FAMILY of New Mexico was large. The patriarch, Elizardo "Lee" Maestas, was also known as Grandpa Lee. He and his wife, Anita, had ten children: Phil, Joe, Isidor, Lee, and Ralph. The daughters included: Agnes, Dora, Anna, Lucy, and Beatriz—the baby. The family lived in Gallina, Cerrillos, and Abiquiu, New Mexico.

To support his large family, Grandpa Lee held several jobs in New Mexico, and later in California. Also, in New Mexico, he owned a coal mine, from which he sold coal, had a gas station in New Mexico, and would later acquire one in California. He was also a forest ranger and worked as a sheep herder for grandma Anita Velarde's family. During the 1930s, he served as the Deputy Sheriff of Abiquiu and the towns of Cerillos and Coyote. A hard worker, for Grandpa Lee, the most rewarding and exciting job he held was that of Deputy Sheriff.

As far as Grandma Anita, similar to women of her time, she was a stay-at-home mother whose primary responsibility was to take care of the children. But, that was not all she did—she was a baker, cook, seamstress, and healer for her family and other people who sought her out. When the Maestas lived in Bernalillo, there was only one doctor for the entire town. Still, as the only doctor he didn't have many patients.

When Grandma Anita saw the doctor walking around town with his medical case, she would say: "There goes the little doctor. He's always walking back and forth, with nothing to do, because we have our own home remedies." Daughter Lucy often recalled that her mother "did everything."

In California, Grandpa Lee purchased a gas station. He also became a mechanic, turning his garage into an auto repair shop.

Grandpa Lee was known as a good provider. He was a good family man and his love was reciprocated by his family. However, like the Kachina dolls of New Mexico, Grandpa Lee was a trickster who loved to tease and play jokes, always searching to get a laugh among his loved ones.

This book tells the story of Grandpa Lee and records the shenanigans he pulled to make light of a hard life. He was truly an extraordinary man.

Cows on the Roof

ON AN ORDINARY MORNING loud sounds originated from the roof of their house, waking up the family. The noise was most pronounced in the boys' bedroom where little Joe asked his brothers: "Do you guys hear strange noises?"

"Be quiet, I'm sleeping," answered Isidor.

The chaos was not limited to the boys' room. In the girls' bedroom, Lucy asked Anna.

"Are you awake? Did you hear anything?"

The noise continued unabated. What was there to do?

Soon enough, the whole family got up. They went to investigate—to see what in the world was happening. Each child went outside and looked up at the roof. To their amazement, they saw a herd of cattle walking on the roof. By this time the entire family was involved in the herd affair. Then, Grandpa Lee and his sons began shooing the cows away and back up on the hill. However, the more they chased the cows, the nosier and louder they became,

mooing here and mooing there. After all the mooing and confusion, on their own the cows slowly turned around, got off the roof, and started back up the hill, although a little calf lagged behind.

Little Lucy wanted to keep the calf, "Papa, can we keep her?"

Grandpa Lee answered, "No, mi hija. He probably belongs to the neighbors, up on the hill."

Grandpa Lee and the children concluded that the cows were grazing downhill because the house was against el barranco or hillside. In their logic, that's how the cattle ended up on the roof, and having nowhere else to go, they stomped around and mooed, as if calling for help—the cows and the families were confused and surprised, until the cows found a way out.

Other surprises or things with which to contend would come to the Maestas' way.

The Falling Viga

EARLY ONE DAY, Grandma Anita was in the kitchen, when she heard baby Lee crying. She stopped what she was doing, went into his room, and picked Lee up from his crib. As Grandma Anita walked toward the kitchen with the baby, she heard a loud bang, which made her younger daughters Anna and Lucy scream—they had been playing dolls in la sala, or living room.

The sound appeared to come from the baby's room. It was time to investigate.

So, with baby Lee in her arms and the younger daughters tagging at her skirt, Grandma Anita, went to the room, opened the door, and found that one of the vigas or beams that supported the roof had come crashing down; it had landed on the baby's crib.

The daughters gasped: "Oh, no!"

Good thing Grandma Anita had taken him out of the crib, when she did. Otherwise, baby Lee would have been seriously hurt or killed by the falling beam.

That evening, when Grandpa Lee returned from work, the boys rushed to let him know about the fallen viga. After listening to the story, he offered that it could have been the weight of the cows on the roof from the day before that brought it down.

He turned to face grandma, telling her, "It's a miracle that you got baby Lee out of there in time."

Grandpa Lee gave Grandma Anita a big hug, asking "What's for dinner? Tengo hambre. I'm hungry."

Food was an important family connection among the Maestas. We loved to eat.

Playing in the Hornos

EVERY SATURDAY MORNING was the ritual by which Grandma Anita provided the family with homemade bread, for the week. It was the day she spent in the kitchen, preparing to bake. She would mix the dough, knead it, let it rise, punch it back down, and repeat the process again, until satisfied that the bread was ready to bake.

When the dough was ready, Grandma Anita would place it in a pan and slide it into the horno—outdoor adobe oven. For this task, she relied on a long wooden shovel-like tool called a "peel."

When the horno was not in use, there were times that the younger Maestas, Anna and Lucy, climbed inside to play house with their dolls. That is, until grandma or one of their older sisters—Dora or Agnes—caught them and chased them out. From the soot inside the oven, the girls were black from head to toe when they came out of the horno. To clean them, Grandma Anita would have to fill a tina or

tin tub with water from the pump, heat the water, and give them a bath. When they were done, the girls would be all clean, while the bath water was pitch black. Sometimes they also took their dolls into the tub.

Anna and Lucy, being close in age, played together often. Along with playing dolls, they enjoyed homemade paper dolls. They cut them out of the Sears and Montgomery Ward catalogs, when Grandma Anita was done, and the

17

sisters would also cut extra clothes. They had fun changing the outfits and acting out different characters. Dolls were their favorite toys.

At Christmas time, they would pray for new dolls. Because the holiday was just around the corner, they waited with much anticipation.

We Don't Want No Kewpie Dolls

WITH THEIR PARENTS, when they went to the department store, the girls picked out the dolls they wanted. Anna would say, "I want the doll with the beautiful blue dress." Lucy would add, "I want the doll with the long dark hair." The next time they went to the store, the girls saw new arrivals and changed their minds.

When Christmas came, the little sisters, Anna and Lucy, received beautiful, new dolls, with long hair and pretty dresses. Their older sisters, Agnes and Dora, got little Kewpie dolls, which were very popular in the early 1920s. However, the older sisters didn't care how popular these dolls were. They were upset because they had gotten little dolls, instead of the bigger, beautiful dolls like their little sisters.

They told everyone who would listen that they didn't want these strange dolls. To prove their point, they held the Kewpie dolls up by their signature curl, at the top of their heads, and dropped them to the ground. On impact, the dolls shattered into tiny pieces. They didn't realize that these strange dolls later would become collectibles.

The Maestas siblings always found ways to play and entertain themselves. One of their favorite games—merging math and eating treats—was called pares y nones or evens and odds. Pine nuts or piñones were used to play the game. Those participating would grab a fistful of pine nuts, and placing them in their closed fists with the hands behind their back asked, "How many do I have?" If the answer was correct, the person who guessed would eat the piñones. If they guessed wrong, the holder of the pine nuts would eat the tasty, roasted treats.

Outdoor activities were always an adventure to be had: playing tag around the well, amusing themselves with the pig, and climbing trees. Lucy appeared to be the most daring of the siblings. One time, she climbed a big tree on the main street, in front of the Cerillos Post Office. She climbed so high, she froze, and could not move or come down. Her siblings sought assistance from an adult to help her. Despite all the fun things to do, among all their activities, playing with their pet pig was the best.

The Pig Named Chico

DURING WINTER BREAK, the children went outside to play in the yard with Chico—their pet pig. They would run and chase him. Chico loved the attention he received from the children. Little Anna especially enjoyed riding on Chico's back, he was like a pony taking her all around the property, until Chico got tired and plopped himself down, refusing to go any further.

One time, when Anna was riding Chico, he stopped so quickly he dumped Anna face down into a puddle of mud. Her brothers and sisters laughed. Lucy told Anna, "I told you Chico didn't like you riding his back."

Anna got up and just turned up her muddy nose. And, with a "humph," went to the water pump to wash the mud off her face.

One day playing with her favorite doll, Lucy went to search for supplies to give her dolly a bath. When she returned, the doll was gone; it was nowhere to be found.

She searched, looked, and looked, and to her dismay she noticed the doll's hair sticking out of Chico's mouth. Enraged, she went after Chico, but there was no hair left in Chico's mouth—he had eaten Lucy's doll.

Beside herself, she chased her pig all over the property, yelling "Chico, come back here. Give me back my dolly."

Chico the pig just ignored Lucy and ran away. Lucy was upset with Chico, because he had eaten the only new toy she received that Christmas time.

Lucy was inconsolable, until Grandpa Lee replaced the dolly with a new one. Then, she was her happy self again. Still, they would take every chance they got to play with their favorite pet.

The Frozen Pet

ONE WINTER DAY the kids went outside to play with Chico. When it got too cold, they all went inside, not realizing they left Chico behind. That evening was very cold. By the time the children remembered Chico was still outside, the pig was frozen.

Tears streaming down their faces, the kids rushed outside and brought Chico into the house. Little Anna was crying the loudest.

"Oh, Chico. My poor baby, Chico," she said, as she cradled the frozen pet. Grandma Anita took Chico from Little Anna's arms. He was so cold, she placed him near the coal stove.

They thought he was a goner. The kids wept because they loved their Chico. Things were so dire, all said a little prayer for their pig.

One by one, the children soon returned to their routines, while frozen little Chico stiffly remained on the rug. Some worked on their homework, while others did their chores.

Sometime later, Chico began to stir. All rushed to his side, to witness Chico coming out of his frozen state.

With her actions, Grandma Anita had thawed Chico back to life. Everyone was happy, especially little Anna, who hugged and kissed her favorite pet until he squealed with delight.

It was a miracle!

Before too long, Chico was back to his old self again. He continued to be a part of their games, as the children chased him around the well of their property. With Chico among the bunch, the kids played and sang "Ring Around the Rosie" and "London Bridge is Falling Down." They gleefully played tag near the wall or chased Chico around and around the well—a place where they all liked to hang out.

Chico and the well

IN THEIR HOME OF ABIQUIU, the Maestas met their daily water needs from a well. Since they didn't have indoor plumbing, the well was their source of fresh water. With the exception of washing clothes, Grandma Anita relied on it the most; for gardening, cooking, bathing the children, and for other chores. However, to wash clothes, she went down to the river with Agnes and Dora in tow. The younger children got fresh water from the well, but also used the well as a play station from which to run around and play tag.

When the lid was not on the well, there were times when the boys acted recklessly and hopped around on top of the brick wall of the well, which was tall enough to protect them from falling in, just to scare their sisters.

Once, when cousins Don, Celia, and Luis Cordova were visiting, all congregated around the well. Then Isidor, showing off for his cousins, offered.

"I bet I could walk on the edge of the well, holding on to Chico."

Don dared him. "I dare you."

"Just watch me," said Isidor.

Without hesitation, Isidor climbed on top of the well's edge. As he held on to Chico, Isidor placed one foot in front of the other. Then, he lost his balance and Chico almost fell into the well!

The sisters screamed. Some cried.

Luckily, Don grabbed Isidor and pulled him down, asking, "Are you guys sure you don't have any missing brothers or sisters around here?"

That was not funny! How could they imagine that Maestas children had fallen into the well?

Goodbye Beloved Pet

THE MAESTAS CHILDREN had years of fun playing with Chico: riding him, dressing him, and giving him treats—he was a member of the family. Everyone in the neighborhood loved Chico. Sadly, he soon turned into a huge swine, which called for Grandpa Lee to put him down. A deed that would be carried out only when the children were out of sight.

Soon thereafter, the deed was done. No one saw a thing.

The day Grandpa Lee took Chico down, he returned home pretending he had just returned from the grocery store. He carried bags full of something, which he placed on the kitchen table, glancing at Grandma Anita with a cocked-eyed look.

Grandma Anita returned the look. Sadly, she was aware that old Chico was the only thing in the bags.

That evening, with the meat Grandpa Lee brought earlier in the day, Grandma Anita prepared the holiday meal, and gave a large portion of meat to the neighbors.

She cooked pork roast, carnitas, and chicharrones—fried pork and pork rinds. The making of tortillas rounded off the meal, as Grandpa Lee recognized Grandma Anita's hard work. And, to lighten the mood, he joked about that one task. "It doesn't matter if the tortillas are perfectly round, they aren't going to roll down into your stomach," he said laughing at his own joke. Grandma Anita ignored him and carried out her tasks. That labor intensive and delicious meal would later be a sad surprise.

Christmas in New Mexico

WHEN GRANDMA ANITA and the older sisters were done preparing the holiday meal, the younger children returned home, having just finished the Abiquiu tradition of going door-to-door, with their "Merry Christmas" greetings, where they got candy at each neighbor's home. Those days, in the little town of Abiquiu, no one dressed up for Halloween or went door-to-door to get candy—this was a tradition for the Christmas season and it would last all day long. Children who came to the Maestas house early in the morning were lucky enough to get Grandpa Lee's hot chocolate and Grandma Anita's biscochitos, for which she was well known. Biscochitos are shortbread cookies with anise and cinnamon and are now recognized as the state cookie of New Mexico.

With their stash of candy, and hungry from all the walking around town, the children were ready to eat. Pork meat, frijoles con chicos, and buñuelos or sugar and

cinnamon coated fried flour tortillas was just the
Christmas feast they needed. The children ate to their
hearts content and were none the wiser. The younger
ones didn't know Chico was on the menu. The older
siblings had their suspicions.

During the holiday season, the family particularly
enjoyed visiting the town of Madrid, New Mexico. That day,
Grandpa Lee would pile the older children into the back
of his GMC truck, while Grandma Anita and the little ones
joined him in the front. They arrived when it was starting to
get dark and in time to take pleasure in the Christmas décor
and holiday lights. Madrid was beautiful!

The town's bosses—The Coal Company of Albuquerque
and Cerrillos—required all the homes to have Christmas
lights and to place a lighted Christmas tree in their front
yard. Toward that end, the coal company gave each
household extra coal the month of December, and would
light up the football field. They had never seen so many
bright lights. The children were in awe of the homes; one
house was more beautiful than the next, and the football
field lights displayed Alice in Wonderland, Pinocchio, and
Cinderella motifs; for the children it was magical.

Each Christmas season, the Maestas children pleaded
with Grandpa Lee to go to Madrid to see the lights. In their
small towns, there was much to do.

Snowball Fight at Recess

NEW MEXICO OFTEN had harsh winters. During the Christmas break, the snow came down very hard. With no choice but to be homebound, there was the day that the family heard a loud rumbling sound—they stopped whatever they were doing and went to the window to witness a snow avalanche barely missing their home. If the house would have been hit, that would have been the end of the Maestas. Their migration to California would not have taken place.

When Christmas break ended, the Maestas children returned to school, and, when it snowed the hardest, students remained in the classroom during recess. Those days, there were no computers or electronic gadgets. So, during inclement weather, the children relied on each other for entertainment. The teacher would ask for volunteers to go to the front of the class and perform. One by one, they raised their hands. Without exception, the children would soon chant, "Anna. Lucy. Anna. Lucy."

By public acclaim, the sisters walked up to the front and sang a duet for the class. As always, they received the loudest applause.

Of course, there were the class clowns. And, one of those boys stood up and announced. "Teacher, teacher, somebody threw a pedo!" The teacher replied, "Well, pick it up and put it on my desk." The entire class erupted in laughter; she had no clue that the children were talking about throwing farts. This was a running joke in New Mexico classrooms, because most of the children spoke Spanish, but many of the teachers only spoke English.

Another day, during recess time, Anna and Lucy were in the playground, playing in the snow, when a group of students started a snowball fight. It looked like fun, so the Maestas sisters joined the bout. As the snowball artillery went back and forth, Anna made a really big, hard snowball, while evading those that came her way. When the snowball was ready, Anna hid her face, closed her eyes, and reached up high, throwing the large snowball as hard as she could. Where it landed did not matter, Anna just wanted to get back at the kids throwing snowballs their way.

At that very time, a yard duty teacher was coming toward them to stop the fight. And, the snowball landed right on her face.

"Who threw that snowball?" yelled the teacher.

Horrified by the incident, Anna confessed. The teacher was upset. As a consequence, Anna missed the next recess.

"Not fair. Why only me?" Anna thought.

There would be other adventures. Other snow playing times would come.

The Ginormous Snowman

IN THE FRONT OF THE MAESTAS HOUSE in Cerrillos, New Mexico, the children came together to make a ginormous snowman. Every day after school, the Maestas kids and their school friends toiled to create their masterpiece. The more they worked, the taller it got, until it became the biggest snowman they had ever seen. It got so large that the children had to use a big ladder to build its head.

It was a delight to build such a huge snowman. Most joyful was when they took breaks to relish their favorite treats or when they savored the delicacies made from the snow they were using to build the snowman. To make this treat, Grandma Anita instructed the children to scoop out white snow from below.

Funny Isidor warned, "Don't use the yellow snow." The children all laughed in agreement.

With their scoops of snow ready, Grandma Anita poured cream with sugar over it—that was their treat. The original snow cone.

Then, when they were done building their snowman, Grandpa Lee gave them a reward. For their efforts, he brewed a big pot of hot chocolate, with pan dulce from El Faro Panadería.

As long as the snow was on the ground, the ginormous art piece became a fixture of the town. At night, with all the luminarias—candles housed in sand-filled paper bags around town—the snowman glowed a shiny white brilliance.

People from other towns drove their children into Cerrillos to witness the children's engineering feat. They went to see the enormous snowman since it would be there beyond wintertime and last until June.

The snowman was loved by all, except for Grandma Anita. For her, it was a great nuisance, because she had to clean the slushy mess left behind. She was a woman of faith and relied on it as necessary.

The Secret Prayer

SCHOOL WAS BUT ONE OF THE WAYS the Maestas kids learned. They also learned from catechism. One day, when Anna and Lucy went to catechism, the teachers instructed them to select a prayer written on a piece of paper, from a large bowl. Each child was told to keep their prayer a secret; it would be their special prayer, and they needed to memorize it and recite it, always. As instructed, Anna and Lucy memorized their prayer and relied on it throughout their lives.

Years later, when they visited each other, the sisters shared their secret. Anna never forgot her prayer. She asked Lucy about that prayer in catechism. That's when they shared their secret prayer. Lucy said it first, and when she was done, Anna chimed in, "that's my prayer, too." They both laughed. After all those years, they finally had found out that those young catechists had given them all the same prayer—what a clever trick that was.

Another day, on a break at catechism class, Anna and Lucy, sitting together to eat a snack, were speaking Spanish. A nun went by and slapped their hands, and scolding them said, "This is America; we only speak English in this country."

The sisters had no clue what they had done wrong. They spoke Spanish at home all the time.

When Grandpa Lee heard about the situation, he went to the church and gave the nun a piece of his mind. He imparted his wisdom on the Sister, telling her this part of the country had been Mexico, insisting that his children could speak the language of their ancestors any time they wished.

Grandpa Lee loved to give advice. His consejos were well known and respected by all who knew him. He always told his children to be proud of whom they were and to honor their two languages.

Ghosts of the Conquistadores

GRANDPA LEE WAS A WISE and smart man. As much as he gave his children advice and warnings, they didn't always listen, and sometimes found their way into mischief. Such as the time when Agnes and Dora, the oldest sisters, went out to the plains, near the coal mine. Grandpa Lee had warned his children not to play out in the plains, and told them to stay away from the coal mine, saying it was dangerous for children to be there unsupervised.

Rashly, these two went to the plains. Then, when the girls played near the entrance of the coal mine, they heard the thunderous sounds of horses galloping nearby. When the clatters got closer, grew louder, it frightened them out of their wits, and the girls jumped into the entrance of the coal mine, just in time to see several men dressed as conquistadores or Spanish explorers riding by on their horses. These eerily and ghostly figures terrified the sisters to the point that they ran all the way home.

When Grandpa Lee saw the girls run into the house, he went and asked them where they had been. As they gasped for breath, both confessed they had gone to the coal mine, and swore they had seen horsemen dressed like conquistadores. Grandpa Lee told them they needn't be afraid, because it was probably conquistador ghosts from long ago, adding "Ghosts cannot hurt you, but that will teach you not to disobey me."

For the sisters, that was the first and only time they went to the plains or near the coal mine by themselves. The Maestas would find alternative ways to enjoy life.

Frogs in the Shoes

EL AGUA ES VIDA, water is life. The Maestas recognized the value of water, and the children loved living near the creek in Cerrillos, where there was also a river, but, as luck would have it, it was further away and would often flood. These floods were announced with a loud roaring sound, which frightened the Maestas children. When the river was dry, the children enjoyed looking out the window to see the puntera or beginning of the flood, to which Grandma Anita said pointing, "Look at the creciente or overflow."

One particular storm, the river overflowed and brought down several houses. The Maestas siblings watched, as their neighbors' homes rushed by. This was a very devastating situation for the neighbors, but the tragedy would inspire the Maestas and their children to help as needed.

The water brought joys and surprises.

One Spring day, little Lucy and Anna were playing outside, when their older sister Agnes asked them to go retrieve her shoes from her friend's house. Her home was a distance away and they would have to cross a small stream to get there. They agreed to go and off they went.

They walked for a while and finally reached the stream. As they crossed it, they had fun stepping on stones, expecting not to fall. Tired of leaping from stone to stone, they finally reached the other side of the stream to continue their journey. They made it to Agnes's friend's house and got their sister's shoes.

As they were heading home, the girls came upon the stream again and noticed that it was filled with tiny frogs. The girls thought the frogs were cute and wanted to take some home. Since they didn't have anything in which to carry the baby frogs, they improvised by using Agnes's shoes, filling each one to the top. So the frogs couldn't escape, each sister held their frog-filled shoe close to their chest. By the time they got home, the shoes were sopping wet.

When they gave the shoes to their sister Agnes, the little frogs jumped out. Agnes looked at the frogs. Then, her wet shoes. But, she wasn't mad at her little sisters, she was just happy they had returned safely. She had been worried about them because they were taking longer than expected. She agreed the frogs were cute. And, the frogs would make the rounds.

The Frog in the Clump

WHEN THE SIBLINGS SAW THE FROGS, the girls
gathered around to play with them, and the boys had frog
races. Then, Grandpa, who was helping Grandma repair the
sala—living room—adobe wall, came out to collect adobe
clay. And, when he saw the frogs, he got an idea. Being the
practical joker that he was, Grandpa Lee grabbed one of the
little frogs and carefully placed it in a large clump of adobe
clay. He went inside. When Grandpa Lee handed the clump
to Grandma Anita, she began to plaster the wall. Slowly, the
little frog jumped out of the clump, and Grandma screamed.
Of course, the children ran inside to see what had happened.

When Grandpa told them what he had done, they
all laughed.

Grandma Anita got mad at him. She was not happy
that he had played that trick on her.

Grandpa Lee never liked it when Grandma Anita was
mad at him, even though he would sometimes be the

cause. However it went, Grandpa would always seek her forgiveness. His best move was to sing her a romantic song. So, when Grandma was in the kitchen, cooking frijoles de la olla con chicos—pinto beans cooked in a pot with sun-dried kernels of steamed corn—Grandpa's favorite, he went up behind her, and began singing Cucurrucucú, Paloma. In a high pitch voice, he sang "Cucurrucucú, Cucurrucucú, Cucurrucucú," and he went higher, and higher, until his voice screeched and cracked, making Grandma Anita laugh.

Still, she would not be easily swayed, and often told him, "Quítate de aquí," or get out of here. In due course, he would get his way.

Another way he had to win her over was with ice cream. She loved ice cream—the whole family loved ice cream. So, when the ice cream man came around, Grandma would give Grandpa a big bowl. He'd go to the ice cream truck to get the bowl filled with scoops of delicious strawberry ice cream. That was but one of the ways Grandma would be rewarded for all the work she did around the house.

Indoor Plumbing

THERE WAS ANOTHER TIME Grandma Anita was upset with Grandpa Lee, and he was trying to sing another romantic song to her. She told him that, if he really wanted her to forgive him, he'd stop singing and do something.

So, he stopped singing and asked Grandma what she wanted. She said that she was tired of getting water from the pump, so he should do something to get her indoor plumbing. Grandpa agreed. He also was tired of going outside to get water, especially during Winter, but he knew that they couldn't afford indoor plumbing.

It wasn't long before he thought of an idea. He would get her water.

So, he went outside, and after tinkering around for a while, he managed to connect the outdoor water pump to the sink in the kitchen. After all the tinkering, he turned the water on and ta-da, they had indoor plumbing. From then on, they never had to go outside to get water again. Nonetheless, Grandpa continued to woo Grandma with his romantic songs.

Hiding in the Rumble Seat

AS MUCH AS GRANDPA LEE DISLIKED Grandma Anita getting mad at him, sometimes he would deliberately tease and upset her. For example, there were those times they had to go somewhere and she rushed him. Well, he'd take his sweet time getting in the car.

"Vámonos, let's go," Grandma would say. But, the more she pushed him, the longer he took. Sometimes, he'd even sit down and get out his pipe, light it, and put his feet up. Then, when he was good and ready, he'd get in the car, sit on the driver's seat, take a few puffs from his cigar, and eventually start the car.

The times they went to Santa Fe was no different. Grandpa and Grandma would go there to buy groceries.

Since Santa Fe was so far and they had a large family, they always bought in bulk, so this left no room in the car to take anyone else. They left the older siblings in charge and drove off. As they were driving off, the children left behind giggled as they waved. The parents waved back, wondering why the children were giggling.

Well, they didn't know what the other children had witnessed. Their little brother Joe had hidden in the rumble seat and had given himself away, peeking out as they drove off. In delight of his antic, they waved and giggled.

Several miles later, Grandpa heard noises in the back of the car. He pulled over to investigate. When he lifted the blankets, he found his youngest son, Joe.

"What are you doing there?" Grandpa Lee asked.

Little Joe smiled. Then, he said, "I'm going to Santa Fe with you and mama."

Since it was too far to go back, little Joe went with them to Santa Fe.

If Grandpa hadn't taken so long to get going—he took his sweet time when Grandma started rushing him—little Joe wouldn't have had enough time to sneak into the rumble seat. Life surely brought unexpected surprises.

In the Middle of the Night

WHEN THEY GOT BACK and unloaded the groceries, Grandma Anita and the older daughters cooked the family meal. When it was ready, they all sat down to eat. Soon after, it was bath time. And, the kids were happiest when they didn't have to go out in the cold to get their bath water.

After bathing, the kids got into their pajamas and sat down at the kitchen table for an evening of storytelling by Grandpa. A great storyteller, he loved to share his stories and all waited with anticipation.

That night he told a scary one.

When all was done, everyone went to bed, all except little Lucy, who had fallen asleep. Grandma didn't want to wake her, so she covered her with a blanket, and left her sleeping on the kitchen bench.

In the middle of the night, little Lucy woke up, and found herself all alone. She didn't know what to do. As their

adobe home was built with exterior doors facing an interior courtyard and all the rooms lacked an exit or entrance to the interior rooms—to get to her bedroom Lucy would have to go outside, but she was scared to go out in the darkness. Finally, Lucy got the nerve to run outside and reached the nearest bedroom, which led to Grandma and Grandpa's door. There, she knocked until Grandpa woke up. He opened the door, picked up his crying child, and took her to her bedroom.

Then, walking back to his bedroom, Grandpa Lee heard a little voice saying, "Daddy, quiero agua. Daddy, quiero agua." In Spanish, four-year old little Joe repeatedly asked for water. Grandpa attempted to ignore his call, heading for his bed. However, before he reached the room, little Joe, in a sad little voice uttered, "Daddy, ya me canse de gritarte—I'm tired of pleading," which made Grandpa turned around. Then, he went to the kitchen, and got little Joe a glass of water. Afterwards, they went back to sleep.

In the morning, as was their practice, Grandpa and Grandma would greet each other and the children with a "buenos días le de Dios." In the event that the children answered without a "le de Dios," Grandpa Lee corrected them. When they responded without that greeting, they would get a scolding such as the time Joe woke up with one eye shut, saying "Me levante con un ojo papado," as if it was covered by a potato, rather than tapado, which meant closed. Grandpa couldn't help but to chortle at his sons misuse of words. He went to get a wet washcloth with warm water and treated Joe's eye. As he washed it, Grandpa exclaimed, "Ave Maria Purisima," a sort of blessing said to someone in need of healing or help.

Grandpa Lee helped in many ways. Other days, he just made life interesting.

Face in the Window

MOST MORNINGS, Grandpa Lee got the coal stove ready. He made a big pot of hot chocolate and one of oatmeal, for the children. When the chocolate and oatmeal were ready, the kids sat at the kitchen table to eat, drink, and talk.

The kitchen was the family's gathering place. All loved to assemble there.

One day, the children were all sitting at the table, eating their meal, and drinking their cocoa. As they ate, Grandpa quietly slipped out. Suddenly, one of children screamed.

"Ayyyyy! It's scary"

The kids looked around to investigate, and they found Grandpa's face smashed up against the window; he looked deformed and scary, which made the rest of the kids scream.

Grandpa relished frightening the children—he loved entertaining them. He always found a way to get one over on them.

Then, there were those times Grandpa Lee made scary sounds. To keep the kids on their toes, he would made scary noises.

No matter how many times he pulled his pranks, without fail, Grandpa Lee got the children to scream. He got a big kick out of it, for sure, but Grandma was there to oversee the mischief. It was she who would come to the kitchen, to remind the children, "It's time to get ready for school."

Mornings at the Maestas were a hoot.

More Mysteries at the Coal Mines

AFTER BREAKFAST, Grandpa Lee would go off to work in the coal mine. During wintertime, he would bring additional coal home for the family's personal stash. The townsfolks knew Grandpa had a coal mine. He sold coal to his neighbors and local businesses. However, there were times he would notice coal was missing in the pile. He would think to himself, "There should be more coal there."

This became another mystery to solve.

So, the next morning, instead of going to the coal mine, Grandpa hid behind the fence. He waited and waited to catch the thief.

Sometime later, he saw a viejito—an old man—with a bucket. Grandpa watched as the old man approached the pile of coal and filled his bucket with as much coal as it could hold. The viejito carefully looked around, hoping no one was watching. Then, in fear of being caught, the old man ran away as fast as his legs would carry him.

Grandpa stayed hidden and just shook his head and laughed. He never confronted the viejito, because he figured the old man must've needed the coal and couldn't afford to pay for it. Grandpa was generous that way.

Sometimes he was a little too generous. Other times, he was a sucker for a hard luck story. If someone needed something he would help, and would even "give away the shirt off his back."

The following week, another mystery connected to the coal mine took place. The Maestas children had a "suspicious meal"—similar to the pork meat—which was served, not only to the Maestas but to the whole school. That day, Grandpa came home from the coal mine, with a whole bunch of meat for Grandma to cook. Because it was more than they needed, Grandma gave most of the meat to the school's cook who used it to make lunch.

The fare was donkey meat, but neither the cook or Grandma Anita realized they were serving burro to everyone.

The family later learned that Grandpa Lee had found a donkey wondering around the coal mine. One of the workers shot it and they divided it up between them. But, the family and students never realized they had eaten donkey meat. In Cerrillos, there were always mysteries to solve.

The Girl in the Hot Springs

OCCASIONALLY, ON THE WEEKEND, Grandpa Lee piled the children into the back of his truck and drove to some fun destination. One of their favorite places was Ojo Caliente, a nearby natural hot springs. He liked going there because it helped soothe his arthritis, and the children loved jumping in and out of the hot water.

When they arrived, the children leapt out of the truck, and before anyone could stop them, they went into the hot water, not noticing who or what may be around. That day, Grandpa saw a girl in the hot springs. Her clothes were spread on the rocks, meaning she was enjoying the hot water in the buff. The girl appeared to be upset, when she saw them. To not add to her discomfort, Grandpa gathered the children and took them back to the truck.

However, before he assembled all of them, the girl jumped out of the hot springs buck naked. She was the color of a red lobster.

As she grabbed her clothes and ran off, the Maestas children howled. Once gone, Grandpa Lee allowed the children to return to the hot springs. From then forward, they had a fun and uneventful afternoon. Grandpa was a friendly and caring sort of chap.

A Friend of the Navajo

TO SUPPORT HIS LARGE FAMILY, Grandpa Lee held many jobs. A hardworking and generous man, when he owned a gas station, he gave credit to those who could not afford to pay for gas. Often, he was not repaid. But, Grandpa never let it bother him.

Grandpa was smart and giving, but he was not really a "businessman." He was more concerned about his family and the community than he was about money. As long as he could support his family, Grandpa was satisfied. For him, having too much or having too many things he didn't need was puro lujo or just luxuries.

With his friends, the local Navajos, Grandpa had ways of doing business; they would barter. The Navajos would give him items, such as blankets or crops such as corn, and he would give them as much gas as they needed. During those cold New Mexico winters, the blankets came in handy.

At the gas station, his Navajo friends would often hang out with him, just shooting the breeze. From time to time, a few of them even worked for him. They taught Grandpa Lee, and uncles Joe and Ralph, to make beautiful silver and turquoise jewelry.

Grandpa would often sing a song in Navajo—more like a chant—to his children, and later to his grandchildren; songs he learned from his friends. There were times my Dad Frank found Grandpa in a room or in the garage, by himself, chanting. He'd ask him what that was all about and he'd say, "something I learned from the Navajos."

Grandpa Lee was indeed a big-hearted man. He was well liked by the Navajo People, and the feelings were mutual.

A New Deputy Sheriff in Town

THROUGH HIS WORK, at his coal mine and the gas station, Grandpa was well-know and liked. He was respected by those who lived in Rio Arriba County. At his gas station, he began to fix cars, which brought more customers. Grandpa was an honorable, brave and fearless man, and a hard worker. So, when there was an opening for Deputy Sheriff of Abiquiu, the townspeople thought of him for the job.

The Marshall asked him to be Deputy Sheriff. Grandpa Lee accepted.

The first time he put on Grandpa Lee's badge, he proudly smiled from cheek-to-cheek, and his children looked at him with much pride. He looked so handsome in his uniform, Grandma even kissed him on the cheek.

As Deputy Sheriff, Grandpa immediately went to work. With the help of a group of men, he set out to build a new jailhouse behind the family home. Grandma wasn't happy about this and told Grandpa so. He said this was the way it had to be. Then, he started singing her a love song, the way he did when he wanted to make her happy. Of course, the song didn't change things—she still didn't like the idea.

When the jail was finished, Grandpa started his assignment as Deputy Sheriff. He was put in charge of investigating the case of a stolen horse from a rancho nearby. Those days, horse thieves were almost as bad as murderers, so it was a serious situation. Without fear and much bravery, Grandpa Lee went about doing the task at hand. He could always solve the case.

On the Case

GRANDPA LEE, AND HIS OLDEST SON, Phil went
to investigate. At the ranch, he looked around for clues.
There in the dirt, Grandpa found a boot print with a
small circular mark on the left sole. Apparently, a pebble
got stuck in the sole of the boot, leading him to believe
it belonged to the horse thief. When he found additional
evidence to identify the suspect, Grandpa went to the
bandit's house.

When Grandpa knocked on the door, the son answered,
and Grandpa asked him to get his father. The son said his
father was asleep. That being the case, Grandpa asked him
to get them. Dutifully, the son brought his father's boots.
When Grandpa examined the soles, he found a pebble stuck
in the exact spot as the boot print he'd found. It was then
that the Deputy Sheriff told the son to have his mother
wake up her husband.

So, he waited and waited. It took longer than expected.

Nearly out of patience, as Grandpa wondered what was taking so long, the husband appeared in the living room. The man's cheeks were bright red. Apparently, to hide his fear, the wife had patted rouge on his cheeks.

Grandpa Lee asked the man where he'd been all evening. "At home sleeping," the man said. He asked him about the fresh dirt on his boots, pointing to the pebble on the left sole, like the one left on the dirt, where a horse was stolen. With evidence in hand, the man confessed he had taken the horse, saying he had sold it. Grandpa inquired as to the horse's whereabouts, the thief didn't know. That was all he needed.

So, Deputy Sheriff Lee Maestas arrested the bandit. Took him to the jailhouse.

By using investigative techniques, Grandpa Lee solved many crimes. He was an original forensic detective, just like those we see on television and the movies. But, he would leave his mark in more than one way.

Bullet Holes in the Ceiling

AMONG HIS DUTIES AS DEPUTY SHERIFF, sometimes Grandpa had to stop men from fighting, even when they were bigger. Grandpa was fearless and did what he had to do. One time, at a local cantina, a brawl broke out and quickly got out of hand. Grandpa was unable to get anyone's attention, so he fired his gun toward the ceiling. With the sound of the shots, everyone stopped fighting. He soon broke it up and everyone went home. To this day and in honor of Deputy Sheriff Elizardo "Lee" Maestas, the cantina has kept the bullet holes in the ceiling.

Grandpa Lee was the only law in town. And, in that capacity, he became a hero to the people of Abiquiu, New Mexico.

Then, there was the time he attempted to arrest a borracho or a drunkard for disturbing the peace. Much larger than Grandpa, the man wrestled Grandpa to the ground. When he couldn't overpower the man, Grandpa bit the man's fingers as hard as he could to gain control. When he handcuffed the guy, Grandpa realized he nearly severed one of the man's fingers. With much compassion, at the jailhouse, Grandpa gave him first aid.

As kind and good as he was, Grandpa Lee was recognized for his fearlessness. As Deputy Sheriff Maestas, he surely would not let anyone control the situation, regardless of their size.

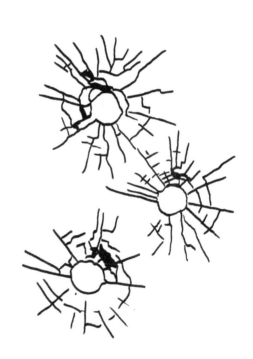

It Was Self-Defense

AS DEPUTY SHERIFF, when a terrible incident occurred in Rio Arriba County, there was a report of a shooting so Grandpa rounded up a posse to arrest the gunman. When they reached the home of the suspect, the man resisted arrest, and fired his shotgun at Deputy Sheriff Maestas who had no choice but to return fire. Two shots and the suspect dropped dead.

Unaware as to why Deputy Sheriff and his posse were at their home, a young person grabbed an old revolver and pointed at Grandpa Lee. Dressed in overalls and with long hair tucked into a baseball cap, Grandpa Lee had no clue that the child was a girl. He fired his gun and hit her left shoulder area, penetrating a lung.

Grandpa felt terrible, and more so when he learned he had hit a young girl. With extra care, he and the posse rushed her to his home to wait for medical assistance. There, Grandma Anita brought out a blanket to give the

young woman comfort, and placing a warm towel over her forehead, she said, "Ave Maria Purisima," to bless the young girl because she would need all the help she could get.
All the girl did was to look at Grandma Anita and say: "Te escapaste de ser viuda or you escaped becoming a widow." Grandma retorted, "las escapadas no duelen or almost don't hurt."

Until the Marshall showed up, the girl stayed in their care. When the Marshall arrived, he rushed the girl to Santa Fe hospital. After an investigation was conducted, it was decided that Deputy Sheriff Maestas was justified in his actions. Witnesses said that the Deputy Sheriff and the suspect were about six feet apart from each other. Since the suspect shot first, it was a miracle that Grandpa Lee wasn't hit.

After finding out what happened, the granddaughter didn't blame Deputy Sheriff Maestas. Grandpa was exonerated. For the difficulty of his work, he would get comfort at home.

Frijoles y Vino

AFTER THINGS SETTLED DOWN, and the investigators completed their job, Grandpa Lee went to the kitchen cabinet to get his "medicine," which is what he called his favorite red wine. He poured himself a glass, and took a big gulp to calm his nerves, as he waited at the kitchen table for Grandma Anita to serve him and his posse New Mexico chili colorado, rice, and beans. She always made his favorite; frijoles de la olla, which he especially liked with Chicos. He didn't like refried beans, and Grandma didn't serve them that way. For him, those were "frijoles mascados, or chewed up beans;" he hated them. In response, Grandma just rolled her eyes.

With much love, Grandpa called his favorite beans "Mexican strawberries." With that, his children would roll their eyes because strawberries were nothing like beans.

When they finished their meal and the posse left, Grandpa said, "Panza llena, corazón contento or full belly happy heart." Then, he took a long nap. Grandma kept the children quiet, telling them to leave Grandpa Lee alone. It had been a very rough day for him.

After this dangerous incident, Grandma Anita begged him to leave his job as Deputy Sheriff. Grandpa loved being a lawman. He could not fathom changing jobs, because he took pride in being the only law in town.

Soon, as much as he loved being Deputy Sheriff, Grandpa began to contemplate a different job. However, Abiquiu, being a small town, lacked employment opportunities. That was when he began to consider relocating his family. This would be something to come.

Who's at the Door?

SOME YEARS LATER, Grandpa Lee took the family to California. They bought a house on Stockton Avenue in San José. It was a big two-story white house, down the street from the well-known Bellarmine Preparatory School for boys. Designated as a mixed area, meaning residential and commercial, Grandpa turned his big detached garage into an auto repair shop. It was then that he honed his craft and earned a reputation for fixing cars—the business was called Maestas Auto Repair Shop. People often would seek him out.

One day, the doorbell rang and Grandpa answered the door. Angel Infante—the brother of the famous Mexican singer and actor Pedro Infante who was famous in his own right—stood in front of him. His limo had broken down near grandpa's house. Angel Infante was lucky. Grandpa was a very good mechanic. In no time, he fixed Angel Infante's limo and he went on his way.

Another time, someone rang the doorbell and Grandpa answered it. When he opened the door, Bing Crosby, the famous Hollywood actor, stood in front of him. Startled to see such a famous celebrity, Grandpa didn't know what to do. So, he just listened.

Apparently, Bing Crosby sons were attending Bellarmine Preparatory. They didn't like the dorms. And, since he had such a big house, so close to the school and assuming the property was a boarding house, Crosby had come to see if his sons could rent a room. Grandpa agreed that it was a big house, "but it's not a boarding house. It's my home and the only people living in it are my family." Told him, "sorry," there was no room for the Crosby boys, Grandpa Lee only had room for his big family. That house held many memories and stored many stories.

Chased with a Rifle

AT THAT BIG WHITE HOUSE, Grandpa Lee and Grandma Anita spent many years raising their children. There were family gatherings for Easter egg hunts, Thanksgiving dinners, and Christmas celebrations, and many other special occasions.

There, Grandpa gained a good reputation for his auto repair shop. He also was known for being protective of his family, especially his daughters.

Soon, before his very eyes, his daughters became teenagers and wanted to date and go to local dances, and the Maestas sisters went to the old Rainbow Ballroom in San José. It was during this time that Mom met Dad at a San José Bees baseball game—at the old stadium on Alma Avenue. He often said, "I took one look at her and that was it."

They started dating, fell in love, and they wanted to get married.

To ask Grandpa Lee for Lucy's hand in marriage, Dad, Frank Najera, went to their home. He was really nervous, when he walked up to the porch and rang the doorbell. Grandpa answered the door and invited the man who would become my father to come in and sit down. There, Frank announced he had come to ask for Lucy's hand in marriage. When Grandpa Lee heard this, he chased Dad out of the house and down the street, aiming a rifle at him.

Back at home, Grandpa yelled that his daughter—she was too young and they hadn't known each other long enough. Needless to say, Grandpa refused to give his blessings.

With this refusal, my parents eloped. Yes, they did.

Now married, they returned home. At first, Grandpa Lee was furious, but then he relented. Until they could buy their own home, he invited them to live in the big white house with the rest of the family. So, they took an upstairs bedroom. Every day, his son-in-law Frank would go off to work, while Lucy helped around the house. Frank was a hard worker and an early riser. So, he usually went to bed early. That got Grandpa to often comment that those who went to bed early were sleeping with the chickens. Ha. Ha. Ha.

Grandpa Lee was a jokester and often tested his mettle with his son-in-law, Frank. One time, when working in his auto repair shop, Frank was looking over his shoulder, wanting to learn more about fixing cars. By this time, Frank had gained the confidence to ask his father-in-law questions.

"How are you going to take that part out?"

Grandpa Lee, feeling that he had asked one too many questions, sarcastically replied, "con mi sombrero y mis pedos or with my hat and the farts I let out." Thus, jokes and other tricks would bond these two men for life.

⎯⎯

I See You Everyday

ONE DAY, WHEN GRANDPA was working on a car in the driveway, Dad saw Grandpa inside waving at him. He waved back and continued up the front walkway. Then, something caught his eye and noticed Grandpa was still gesturing. So, Dad returned the greeting, thinking, "Gee, he's really happy to see me." Still, Dad continued walking, then Grandpa waved more vigorously, to which Dad responded more enthusiastically. This time, Grandpa's face was contorting and turning red, as if yelling something at Dad. Since all the windows were up and because Dad couldn't hear him, he went to check on Grandpa. When Dad got closer, Grandpa signaled him to unlock the car.

When Dad opened the car door, Grandpa shouted, "Pendejo, couldn't you see that I was locked inside the car?"

Dad's replied, "You were waving so much, I just thought you were happy to see me."

Grandpa retorted, "Idiota, why would I be so happy to see you. I see you every day."

At that, Dad shrugged his shoulders and headed in the house. As soon as Dad entered, he was laughing so hard, Mom asked, "What's so funny?" When he started telling her, Grandpa entered the house, and asked, "What's so funny?" With a straight face, Dad said, "Nothing."

After Grandpa walked away, Dad finished telling Mom what had happened. They doubled up with laughter; they just couldn't help themselves.

Grandpa heard them and said, "I don't see anything funny about it." Later, he told Grandma Anita what had happened. She tried not to laugh, but also saw it as funny. Then, they both cracked up.

Grandpa Lee was more than the life of the party. He always kept things interesting.

—

Do You Think You're Strong?

EVERYONE LIKED TO VISIT our home to hang out with Grandpa Lee, not just his sons but his sons-in-law, too. As well, my Dad's brothers enjoyed visiting him.

What's not to like? He was friendly, intelligent, funny, and entertaining. Grandpa Lee told stories and gave advice.

One afternoon, my Dad brought his brother Jim over to the house. After Dad introduced him, Grandpa asked him if he thought he was strong. "Sure," Jim replied. So, Grandpa told him to lift up the motor that he had in the garage. Uncle Jim said he thought he could. So, they went into the garage and Grandpa put the motor on a strap and got it ready. Jim, with his strong arms, lifted the motor off the strap and put the motor down.

Without saying a word, Grandpa tightened the belt around the motor, put the strap in his mouth and with his teeth he lifted it and set it down. In awe of him, Uncle Jim told Grandpa: "You win." Just then, Joe and Ralph walked up to meet Frank's brother, Jim who began telling them how strong Grandpa was. For them it was not unusual, they had seen Grandpa Lee do that as long as they could remember. When uncle Jim was leaving he told my father.

"Your father-in-law, that sucker is strong."

Grandpa liked to show his strength. He got a kick out of the reactions he would get when he showed off his vigor.

His sons were good-natured and got along well with their brother-in-law, but when they first met him, they weren't so sure about him.

When Isidor and Phil first laid eyes on him, he was dressed in a nice, fancy Zoot Suit—Dad was proud of his semi-drapes what they called that style in the barrio. The brothers whispered to each other, "es pachuco— a street-wise flamboyant playboy."

He was not a pachuco, he just liked being well-dressed. Then, Isidor said, "Guarda pedos, esos pantalones are fart savers."

With that, they all started laughing. Even my Dad.

Isodor, however, would needle his brother-in-law.

"¿Por qué vienes vestido de payaso? Why are you dressed like a clown?"

To tease him. Phil asked, "Has your Mom seen you dress like that?"

"No." Frank said, "I always change before I get home."

One of my aunts heard her siblings tease my Dad about the way he dressed, she shrugged her shoulders, saying "Así es Kiko or that's Kiko"—that was my Dad's nickname.

For Grandpa Lee everybody was family, including friends and neighbors. Each and every one was there to make life easy.

The One-Armed Man

GRANDCHILDREN WERE ALWAYS AROUND; at one
time or another, some even lived with our grandparents.
Whenever there was a family celebration, like a baptism
or wedding, all gathered at their home. But, Sundays were
the times that grandchildren loved best. All looked forward
to the gettogethers and playing outside in front of their
Stockton Avenue home. Later, they would meet at their
house near the Willow Glen area of San José, California.

One day, at the Stockton Avenue house, the grandchildren
were playing in the front yard. Grandpa Lee's friends, a man
named Willy, was helping him work on a car in the driveway.
Willy had an artificial arm, and while working with Grandpa
Lee, he exposed it. As they talked about what was wrong with
the car, a few of the grandchildren came running around the
corner of the house, playing tag. When they looked at Willy's
arm, they stopped in their tracks, screaming they ran in the
opposite direction.

Their reaction irritated Willy, who told Grandpa Lee.

"Why do you teach your children to be afraid of black people? I thought you were my friend."

Upset to hear that, Grandpa Lee replied, "I AM your friend. I didn't teach them to act that way. My grandchildren have never seen a man with an artificial arm. They just got scared and ran."

Grandpa Lee and his friend Willy looked at each other and broke into a hardy laugh. They continued to work.

The Steering Wheel Won't Turn

DAD BOUGHT A YELLOW 1942 Lincoln convertible. He took it to Grandpa Lee to do a test drive and to check it out.

For the test drive, Grandpa Lee insisted on taking the car for a spin by himself. So, they stayed on the sidewalk and watched, as Grandpa got into the Lincoln and started driving. As the car moved down the road, Dad and uncle Ray walked along the sidewalk. Grandpa was moving along fine, then he began yelling, "the steering wheel won't turn" just as he was heading toward a pole. Not being able to stop the car, he was lucky the car didn't crash. My Dad and uncle Ray ran over to where he was, and as Grandpa got out of the Lincoln—the two of them couldn't help but chuckle.

Grandpa demanded to know why the car wouldn't turn. He could not understand why that happened.

My Dad answered, "The Lincoln has a new thing called an automatic transmission and you need to turn the key, not just the starter button, to get the steering wheel to work."

With an annoyed look, Grandpa Lee said, "Why didn't you tell me that before I started driving it?"

"I tried to tell you before you got in the car, but you interrupted and said you knew everything there was to know about cars," came Dad's reply. In the brink of laughter, the two men held it down; they knew better than to laugh at Grandpa's face, anyway.

All recognized that Grandpa was a great mechanic. That he knew much about cars. However, with the new transmissions, he had much to learn. My Dad shared a love for fixing cars with Grandpa. And, he particularly enjoyed watching Grandpa at work, especially when he poked his head under the hood, to ask questions.

He liked his son-in-law, but, sometimes, Grandpa ran out of patience with him. Once again, when Dad had his head under the hood, and he had asked one too many questions, Grandpa Lee let the hood fall knocking Dad on the head.

Dad learned much from hanging around at Grandpa Lee's auto repair shop. And, he became a good mechanic himself. Cars and family issues would unite the family during good and bad times.

Very Sad News

AFTER THE WAR ENDED, the Maestas anxiously awaited Lee Jr's return. One day, while Grandpa and Grandma sat in the kitchen having coffee, there was a knock at the door.

Grandpa opened the door. Two men were standing in front of him. They wore their formal military uniform. When Grandma saw them, she began to cry—she knew it wasn't good news.

Grandpa invited them inside the house. They sat in the living room.

In haste, the men told them that their son, Lee Jr. had died. Without details, they told my grandparents how sorry they were, and left.

My Dad Frank and uncle Ray followed the men out the door, asking if they knew what had happened. All they knew was that he had fallen off the train in Germany. Again, they expressed their condolences, without providing additional information.

Shortly thereafter his body was flown to the United States. Lee Jr. survived the war, but somehow died on his way back home! This mystery would remain unsolved.

Those days, people took the military at their word. No one questioned what happened.

Secretly, however, they all had many questions. Queries that were never answered.

The family held funeral services for Lee Jr. where all gathered to honor the soldier that had proudly served his country. Relatives as far away as Utah, New Mexico, and Colorado came to pay their respects. Grandma was comforted to have her sisters, Romelia and Amalia, with her. During these difficult times, her niece Mary came to stay.

As the family grew and started their own families, they moved into their own homes. Visits became less frequent.

Gatherings in the New House

WITH THE CHILDREN GROWN and with families of their own, the white house on Stockton Avenue was too big for my grandparents. So, they decided to make new memories in a new home, even though they would be leaving a place that stored memories for all.

When they shopped around for a house, the realtor refused to show them houses in the Willow Glen area of San José, even though they could have easily afforded to buy one in the coveted area. Because of their heritage, it appeared the realtor was discriminating against them. So, they settled for a nice home near Willow Glen, where Grandpa Lee would buy a gas station nearby.

As was their tradition, every Sunday, the extended family came together at our grandparents' new home, just as we did at the big white house on Stockton Avenue, where the grandchildren played and had fun times. Just like his children, the grandchildren could not help but get into mischief.

At the new house, there was a creek in the back. The children had much fun playing there, even when they were restricted from going. Other times, they snuck off to the store, which was a few blocks away, to buy candy and sodas and we'd always get a Coca Cola for our oldest cousin Carla. But, most of the time, we played for hours in front of the house—we had fun times.

One Christmas time, we gathered at our grandparents' home, and while the women were in the kitchen making tamales, biscochitos, buñuelos, and other holiday treats, the grandchildren remained in the living room anxiously awaiting their presents. It was tradition to open them at midnight.

However, it was that year that Grandpa proclaimed we would open our gifts an hour before midnight. That was great news for us. We all got extremely excited. Our oldest cousins, Dolores and Carla, had to calm us down with Christmas carols. As we waited for the clock to strike 11:00 pm, the singing got more spirited and louder as the time got nearer, even though it appeared to slow down, and it took forever, but we finally could open our presents. As if approaching the finish line, we all rushed to the presents, and began peeling the wrapping paper. All were overjoyed.

Great memories were made at our grandparent's house. In the morning, after all the Christmas festivities, Grandpa made his grandchildren a big pot of hot chocolate and an even bigger pot of oatmeal, like he did when his children were small.

As he had done with them, Grandpa Lee quietly sneaked out. As his grandchildren ate, drank, talked, and laughed, one of the grandchildren screamed at the vision. All turned to see Grandpa Lee's face smashed against the window.

Across generations, no matter how many times he pulled that trick, Grandpa caught his grandchildren off guard. Sometimes, before pressing his face against the window, he would wrap a lady's scarf around his head, hoping we wouldn't recognize him.

Grandpa loved to surprise his grandchildren, just as he did his own. He was a fun grandpa. And, he was dearly loved by his entire family.

In many ways, Grandpa Lee made life interesting and fun. He had a big heart, and in his grandchildren's eyes, he was larger than life.

Grandpa Lee is Gone

AT THE AGE OF SEVENTY-THREE, Grandpa was in his garage, working, as usual. He was fixing a washing machine and a dryer. At the time, I was in college, and because he was scheduled for open-heart surgery, I'd stopped for a quick visit. When I walked into the garage, he peeked to see who it was, and greeted me.

"Hi, mi hija. Buenos días le de Dios."

Forgetting to respond in kind, as was the tradition, I said. "Hi, grandpa. You sure know how to fix a lot of things."

"You're such a hard worker. Don't you ever get tired?" I asked.

Without hesitation, scolding me for breaking tradition, Grandpa Lee replied. "There is always so much to do. I like to keep busy."

Then, he got up to give me a hug and kissed me on the cheek. As always, he gave me a bit of advice.

As I turned to leave, he said. "Stay in school and finish college."

"I will grandpa. Love you. Bye," I replied.

"I love you, too. Goodbye." Grandpa Lee uttered.

I walked out the door and drove away. And, I returned to my dorm at San José State University.

Six days later, Grandpa was in the hospital with an enlarged heart. They were operating on him, so the whole family went to support him. There were so many of us, the waiting room was crowded—a testament to the love our family had for Grandpa.

After visiting for a while, the cousins got hungry, so we asked if we could go get something to eat. My Mom told us that the doctor said the surgery was going well. We should go eat lunch. With her blessing, we piled into several cars and found a restaurant.

We had the best time. It felt wonderful to be with family.

As we waited, since, we had gone our separate ways in life and had not gotten together in quite a while, we reminisced and talked about how much we loved Sundays at our grandparents. After two hours of eating, talking and laughing, we returned to the hospital.

We parked the cars. And, walking toward the entrance we ran into uncle Ralph. Crying, he told us. "Your grandpa is gone," turning away from us he continued sobbing.

In disbelief, we all rushed to the elevators, to the surgery waiting room, where we found the family in tears, comforting each other. That's when we all realized it was true. Our beloved Grandpa had passed, while all the cousins were away having a good time at lunch. Each one of us felt guilty, but aunt Agnes reminded us that Grandpa would have wanted it that way.

Throughout our lives, Grandpa Lee and Grandma Anita always hosted family events. Now, we were here saying our good byes. We would surely miss him.

Epilogue

FOR MY FAMILY AND ME, Grandpa Lee was an inspiration in many ways. A great storyteller. A man of the law who provided his family a good life, always dispensing his humor and going about his jokester ways.

As his granddaughter, I have been inspired to write his stories. To record the memories of those who knew him and experienced his sense of humor and his love of life. Privileged to hear stories from my grandmother, mother, father, and aunts and uncles, I share them to keep his legacy alive.

While oral history is one way to make visible these common experiences, I have put pen to paper to narrate some of his shenanigans for all to enjoy. I urge each and every one of you to write your family legacies.

In his honor, I close with the lyrics for a ballad I wrote for him.

Ballad of Grandpa Lee

GRANDPA LEE WAS A DEPUTY, BACK IN ABIQUIU

HE RODE WITH A POSSE,

CATCHING OUTLAWS IS WHAT HE'D DO

THE JAILHOUSE WAS OUT IN BACK

AND WHEN HE HAD TO USE HIS GUN

GRANDMA AND THE CHILDREN WOULD
DUCK FOR COVER OR RUN

ONE WARM NIGHT, GRANDPA LEE SAT
ON HIS PORCH ALL NIGHT

WAITIN' FOR THE MARSHALL,

TO TAKE THE OUTLAW HE'D LOCKED UP TIGHT

WELL, GRANDPA DOZED OFF AND WHEN HE WOKE,

A GUN WAS POINTED AT HIS HEAD

HE GRABBED HIS GUN, AIMED, FIRED
AND SHOT THAT STRANGE MAN DEAD

WHEN THE STRANGER WENT DOWN,

HIS HAT FELL OFF AND ALL HIS LONG HAIR SPILLED

GRANDPA LEE WAS STUNNED TO SEE,
IT WAS THE OUTLAW'S DAUGHTER

HE KILLED

GRANDPA HAD LOTS OF STORIES TO TELL
OF THINGS THAT HAPPENED

LONG AGO

THIS STORY IS SAD, BUT IT'S TRUE AND IT HAPPENED
IN NEW MEXICO

GRANDPA LEE WAS A DEPUTY, BACK IN ABIQUIU

HE RODE WITH A POSSE,

CATCHING OUTLAWS IS WHAT HE'D DO

 **HELEN NAJERA REYES** was born and raised in San José, California. She is a retired reading specialist and classroom teacher, with more than thirty years of experience. She wrote this book, with the hope of inspiring every person—family historian—to write the stories of their families. Najera Reyes wrote and recorded Ballad of Grandpa Lee in 1992, to document the shooting incident of 1931 told in the text. She has nearly reached her silver anniversary of marriage to Gabriel Allan Reyes, with whom she shares the love and care of their grandchildren. They volunteer their time in the cultural life of Morgan Hill, California, where they raised their four daughters, and continue to reside.

A flourishing independent artist, **HECTOR GARZA** has been a dedicated educator for the last fifteen years in San Antonio, Texas. He has a BA in Art with a Minor in Music from Our Lady of the Lake University, an MA in Education from the University of Notre Dame, and an MFA in Painting from the Savannah College of Art and Design. Fall of 2019, Garza was accepted into the Institute for Doctoral Studies in Visual Art where he is completing his PhD. Garza is an Academic Success Coach at Our Lady of the Lake University and is a professor of Sacred Art and Architecture at the Mexican American Catholic College.

CPSIA information can be obtained
at www.ICGtesting.com
Printed in the USA
FSHW020821231120